Love Letters:

From His Heart to Yours

30 days of devotional encouragement

Cindy Powell

Published by Simple Faith Press,
P.O Box 1614, Redlands, CA 92373

All Scripture quotations, unless otherwise indicated, are taken from the Holy Bible, New International Version®, NIV®. Copyright © 1973, 1978, 1984, 2011 by Biblica, Inc.™ Used by permission of Zondervan. All rights reserved worldwide. www.zondervan.com The "NIV" and "New International Version" are trademarks registered in the United States Patent and Trademark Office by Biblica, Inc.™ Copyright © 1973, 1978, 1984 by International Bible Society. Used by permission of Zondervan Publishing House.

ISBN-10: 1543168647

ISBN-13: 978-1543168648

To the One who always speaks to my heart with such tenderness and love.

Table of Contents

Introduction

I love receiving mail. Real mail, that is. You know, something encouraging and personal, as opposed to just bills and advertisements! I also happen to love hearing the voice of God. His is the most beautiful and encouraging voice I've ever known. So what could be better than daily "mail" directly from His heart to our own? That lovely thought is the concept behind *Love Letters: From His Heart to Yours.*

God loves to speak to His beloved (that would be you) but often we are too distracted to hear Him. However, when we do take the time to slow down and listen, He is always ready to meet us.

The words on these pages of are the result of taking a few moments to slow down and listen to His heart. Many of these "Love Letters" came as a response to my need to hear His voice for myself, but other times I simply asked what was on His heart and leaned in to listen.

This book contains thirty of those messages—each one a precious message from His heart to the heart of His beloved. In addition to the words I sensed Him speaking, each entry also contains a relevant scripture, a few devotional thoughts regarding the day's topic, and, finally, a short prayer.

In learning to hear the voice of God, we all develop our own unique "language" with Him. The words on these pages reflect the way He speaks to *me*. As a result, I realize the words may resonate most with those who share a similar spiritual vocabulary. However, regardless of the language you personally use with the Lord, my sincere desire is that the words I've recorded will be a spark that causes you to explore His heart more deeply for yourself.

My prayer is that these devotions will be a tool that helps you slow down for a few moments each day to lean into His heart. Because His heart is *always* longing to connect with yours.

Day 1

But Jesus often slipped away to be alone
so he could pray.
—Luke 5:16 (NCV)

My heart is calling out to you, beloved. Take a deep breath—right here, right now, right where you are. Tell your racing thoughts to settle down for just a moment. Quiet your soul and come to Me. Place your ear on My chest and simply listen—listen to the beating of My heart. Hear the rhythm of My love. It's steady. It's strong. It never wavers. Draw strength from the unrelenting strength of My love.

Draw close little one—I'm already nearer than you think. Steal away from the busyness of the day—from the constant demands on your time—and lean into

Me. Whenever you stop to listen, even in the midst of the commotion that often fills your days, you will hear my Spirit calling. In the stillness, in the silence—I am here. I am with you. Hear the tender whispers of My love. As you allow My love to wash over you, I will refresh and restore your soul. There is life in My voice. There is peace in My Presence. There is acceptance in My gaze—so look to Me.

I am always waiting. I am always watching. I never grow weary or restless. I am always accessible and available—and I long to be with you anytime and anywhere. Quiet your soul, beloved, and be still. Be still and know that I am God.

If the Son of God Himself needed to take time alone to quiet His soul and commune with the Father, how much more do we need to do the same? But the reality of our busy lives means most of us don't get nearly as much "quiet time" as we need. While nothing can take the place of those blissful, unhurried times of lingering in His presence, we don't need to wait until we have hours to spend before slipping away to be alone with Him. We are living, breathing houses of prayer. We are walking tabernacles of His Presence. Sometimes all it takes is a moment of looking upward to tap back into that reality. When we are rightly aligned with the unhurried flow of heaven, a single moment of stillness becomes an eternal moment—a holy moment. So take a deep breath—where you are right now—and slip away with Him. Allow Him to lead you beside still waters. He *will* restore your soul.

Lord, thank You for the unchanging reality of Your presence. Thank You for the deep restoration I find in You—anytime, anywhere. Help me, Lord, in the busyness of my life, to still the commotion and simply look up. Be my quiet place, Lord—be my peace. Make this moment holy as I lift my gaze to You. ~Amen.

Day 2

A bruised reed he will not break; a smoldering
wick he will not snuff out. In faithfulness,
he will bring justice.

—Isaiah 42:3

I see you, little one, I see you. I know your heartache. I've felt your pain. I know the injustices you've suffered at the hands of others. As you've wept, I've wept with you. Not a single tear has escaped My notice. Through the dark and lonely nights when you could not feel My Presence, I was there. Unseen arms held you close through the darkest hours of the night. I have never been against you—I am always for you. Though you felt abandoned, I never left your side. For a moment—just for a moment—you may have lost sight of Me, but I have never taken My eyes off of you.

I know the night has been long, but it is coming to an end. The hope of a new day is on the horizon! The sun is rising—and you, too, will rise. You have waited and you have endured—now you will arise. You will soar above the battle on the wings of eagles. The heights of your victory will be far greater than the depths of your despair. This is not an end, it is a brand new beginning. Your future is bright with promise! Hand-in-hand, we will walk into the future together. And I promise to never leave your side. Ever.

There is no compassion greater than the compassion of our God. No one has a greater understanding of heartache, rejection, suffering and loss than our Savior. He will never kick us while we're down. He will never—*ever*—exploit our vulnerability. He gets it. He gets *us*. He knows when we're weak and weary. He knows when we feel like we can't take another step. We don't have to pretend to have it more together than we really do—He already sees the truth. But He also sees the end from the beginning and He knows that *no* night lasts forever. The sun will rise. Hope will rise. And joy *will* come in the morning.

Lord, thank You for new days, new seasons, and the promise of new life! No matter how long the night has been, joy still comes in the morning. Thank You for Your faithfulness in every season. ~Amen.

.

Day 3

You have stolen my heart, my sister, my bride;
you have stolen my heart with one glance
of your eyes.

—Song of Solomon 4:9

ow I long for you, beloved one—how My heart aches for you. You (yes, you!) are the desire of My heart and the object of My affections. Each and every time you look My way, My heart is overwhelmed with love and longing. Your love thrills Me—you have captured My heart!

Each time you think of Me, each time your heart moves in My direction—My heart leaps toward you. I know your thoughts and I know your desire to please Me—that in itself pleases Me more than you will ever comprehend. *Even when you question your motives and wonder about the depth and sincerity of your love, I still believe in you. I know your love is real.*

Yes, you are still growing and learning My ways. Yes, you still falter at times. But moments of weakness never cancel out the true longing of your heart. You judge yourself based on how you perceive the results of your devotion, but I have always looked upon your heart. And your heart is Mine, beloved. Now, always, and forever—I am yours and you are Mine. And come what may, My desire will always be for you.

Just think of it—the Creator of the Universe is in love with *you*! He doesn't just *love* you—He is madly, passionately, head-over-heels *in* love with you! You are the object of His burning desire and fervent affections. His love is so relentless and passionate that He was willing pay absolutely any price to redeem you. He was pursuing your heart long before you gave Him a passing thought. But when you finally looked His way—oh, how it thrilled His heart! Even in imperfection and weakness— even as you're "working it out"—your love still moves Him. Your affection still delights Him. Your companionship captivates Him. Truly, the King is enthralled by your beauty and you've stolen His heart with one glance of your eyes!

Lord, open our hearts to know—really know— how much you cherish our love. Even though our love is weak and imperfect, it is the joy and delight of Your heart. May that stunning knowledge spur us on to love you even more. ~Amen.

Day 4

"Lord, if it's you," Peter replied, "tell me to come
to you on the water."

"Come" he said.

Then Peter got down out of the boat, walked on
the water and came toward Jesus.

—Matthew 14:28-29

*I see you watching the waves and wondering—
do I dare? Do I dare to risk it all? Do I dare to
risk it all...again? I see the fear and trembling
in your heart. I see you counting the cost. But I also see
something else: I see faith. And your faith pleases Me.*

*I know it's frightening, but I also know that you
already know what to do. Even more, I know you've
already made your choice. Put your hand in mine,*

beloved, gaze steadfastly into My eyes—and take a leap of faith. Step out onto the waves. Don't look back upon past failures and don't look down upon your own inadequacy—look ahead. Look at Me. As You walk with Me, the impossible becomes possible.

You were created for more than the ordinary. You are My workmanship and I fashioned you to be extraordinary. New adventures await you, little one. I know you thought you may have missed your chance, but our journey together is just beginning! Don't put it off a minute longer! If you keep your eyes on Me, I promise that you'll do more than walk on water. Together, we'll dance upon the waves.

It's hard to risk. Especially when you've already taken a few significant leaps of faith and things didn't turn out exactly as you hoped. It's easy to back down; to look for an easier path. It's natural to want to be self-protective. But when you truly spend time with the *super*natural Creator of the Universe, it becomes pretty hard to settle for what is merely natural. When you gaze into eyes of fire, they draw you in. Just one glimpse into *those* eyes and all of a sudden, the impossible seems possible...again.

When your eyes are on Him, it's much easier to forget about *your* failures and *your* inadequacies, because you realize His grace and strength are wholly sufficient for every need. So go ahead—take His hand. Gaze steadfastly into those beautiful eyes and take a leap of faith...yet again.

You won't be sorry.

Lord, thank You for the grace to step out in faith...again. And thank You for the faith to believe I really will learn to dance upon the waves with You. ~Amen.

Day 5

The Lord turned to him and said, "Go in the
strength you have and save Israel out of Midian's
hand. Am I not sending you?"

—Judges 6:14

*My precious, beloved child, I love your
fierce commitment to the things of My
kingdom. I love that you want to do all
things with excellence, and that you long to be prepared
and ready whenever I call. But don't you see that your
entire life has served as preparation? All of the
preceding years have prepared you for this specific
moment in time. So walk through the doors I've set
before you with confidence. Go forward without fear
and without hesitation. I am with you.*

I know you feel weak. I know the trembling in your soul. But I have always been, and will always be, your strength in weakness. Go in the strength you have—no matter how small it may seem—because I am the One who is sending you.

Thank you for simply saying yes. My eyes search to and fro for those who will say yes to the desires of My heart. I've found that yes in your heart, and because I have, I am sending you in the fullness of My blessing and power.

Ever feel like God calls you when you're at your very weakest? When you couldn't possibly *feel* any less ready–that's when He seems to think it's the perfect time to send you out. He is always challenging us to move beyond our comfort zones and beyond those places *we* think we're ready to go. In those moments we have no one to lean on but Him–and I'm pretty sure He likes it that way! If you sense the call of God in a particular area of your life but don't feel quite ready–go anyway. Don't wait another minute. Go in the strength you have, regardless of how small that strength may be. Let your confidence be in Him. If He has sent you, you're ultimately going in His strength and *not* your own. And in His strength—*all* things are possible.

Thank You Lord, that Your power really is made perfect in my weakness! Help me to simply say yes when you call, knowing You are able to finish all You've started in me. ~Amen.

Day 6

How precious to me are your thoughts, O God!
How vast is the sum of them! Were I to
count them, they would outnumber
the grains of sand.

—Psalm 139:17-18

I never stop thinking about you, beloved—
you're always on My mind. And every single
one of My thoughts toward you are good! My
intentions toward you are good—always. My
hopes and dreams for you are beyond anything you've
yet to imagine. Sometimes you think your own dreams
are too big, but you haven't yet begun to dream big
enough! All things are possible for Me—and all things
are possible for those who believe.

18

There is a place in My plans—a special place no one else can fill—waiting just for you. There is a place you fit. It's not too late and you haven't missed it. It's true that your own choices matter, yet I left nothing to chance. I knew all the roads you'd choose from the beginning. All your days were written in My book before one of them came to be. Every past season, all the circumstances of your life, have been stepping stones leading you to this very hour. I won't fail you—and you won't fail Me.

I believe in you, beloved. I believed in you long before you believed in Me, and I will always believe in you. So dream with Me. Trust Me with abandon. I promise, the best is yet to come!

Can you imagine all of the grains of sand on one small stretch of beach? How about the grains of sand in just one small fistful? No? Neither can I! But God can and that's how often He thinks about *you*! His thoughts toward you are infinite—there is never a time you are not on His mind. He is never too busy. He is never more concerned about someone or something else. He literally has all the time in the world for you. And every time He thinks of you—

and remember how often that is—He smiles. He knows exactly what He created you for and He knows the dreams and desires He's had for you from the beginning. He also knows *your* dreams and desires—and He wants to share them with you.

Why not take Him up on it? Why not dare to dream with God? Dare to dream with the One whose thoughts toward you are so wonderfully, marvelously, extravagantly, outrageously good. The sky's the limit!

Lord, thank You for believing in me and for inviting me to dream with You. Truly there is no limit on the dreams I can dream with You! ~Amen.

Day 7

"He who believes in Me, as the Scripture said,
'From his innermost being will flow rivers
of living water.'"

—John 7:38 (NASB)

My sweet persistent child, I love your enthusiasm! I love that you want to please Me and always want to do what is right in My eyes. You keep asking Me what I want you to do, but right now I don't want you to "do" anything—I just want you to "be." I want you to be still and be with Me. I want you to be still and know you are mine—and I am yours. It's good that you know and believe faith requires action, but true faith in action is doing whatever I ask you to do—even when

I'm simply asking you to be. There are times it requires more faith to rest than to act. It is only in learning to "be" that you will ever fully know when and what to "do."

I love that you always want to try harder and that you want to learn from your "mistakes" when you feel that, perhaps, you haven't done something as well as you should have. You don't give up and that is one of My favorite things about you! But you will never lay hold of My heart and purposes by trying harder—some things happen only by being. Because when you take the time to be, rivers of living water will flow out of your innermost "being" in ways that can never be accomplished by "trying."

I love you beloved one. Put all your trying aside for a moment and simply be. Rest in Me. Trust Me. As you do, you'll find My life flowing through your own in the most unexpected and delightful ways.

It's hard to let go. Sometimes it is hard to simply rest and trust. Everything in us wants to try, and try, and keep on trying, until we get it just right. But what if that isn't the goal? What if it *does* take more faith to "be" than to "do"? What if abiding in Him really is the key to fruitfulness and to abundant life? What if He really is more interested in our companionship and in simple faithfulness than in a list of accomplishments—no matter how noble they may be?

Sometimes we need to slow down, take a deep breath, rest in His arms—and just *be.* As we lean into His presence and realign our hearts with His, the continuous, effortless flow of heaven *will* flood through our lives.

Lord, thank You for the rivers of living water that flow abundantly from Your heart through my own. Help me to remain in sync with You and the unforced rhythms of Your grace for all of my days. ~Amen.

Day 8

Those who look to him are radiant; their faces
are never covered with shame.

—Psalm 34:5

*S*et your gaze above, beloved; fix your eyes on
Me. Let the light of My love fill you and chase
away all remnants of the night. The darkness
is behind you. Truly it is a new season and a new day!
You are a new creation in Me; old things have passed
away—all things have become new. This isn't about
what you feel; it's about who you are—and you are
Mine!

Whenever you feel shame over the things you've
done in the past—or for the things you've failed to
do—that is never My doing. I never look upon you

with disappointment or regret. All of your sin and failures were washed away by the blood I shed on Calvary. Whenever you fail or feel defeated—look up. You will always find acceptance and love in My eyes. My arms are always open to you and I am never ashamed to call you My own—never! Look to Me, beloved one—when you do, the light of My countenance will always shine upon you and give you peace.

We may fail, but His love never does. One the most astounding personal revelations we can receive is that God's love and acceptance is never—*ever*—conditional. Never! His love is *never* based on our "performance." David—the man after God's own heart—failed again and again, but he learned to run *to* the Lord in his brokenness and failure rather than *away* from Him in shame and regret. Oh how we need to do the same! All shame and regret melt into peace in the radiance of His Presence. In Christ, *nothing* can separate us from His love. Nothing ... *ever!*

Lord, may the revelation of your unconditional and unending love invade our hearts and lives like never before. May we rest so securely in Your love and acceptance, that nothing moves us from that amazing place of grace. Truly, nothing can separate us from Your love! ~Amen.

Day 9

There is no fear in love. But perfect love drives
out fear, because fear has to do with
punishment. The one who fears is
not made perfect in love.

—1 John 4:18

I see your heart, beloved one—and I see the
hearts of the ones you long to protect. I see the
ones you long to speak up for and the ones you
want to defend, but have you forgotten I love them more
than you do? Have you forgotten I am with them and
for them in ways you can never be? Yes, I've called you
to be a voice for the voiceless—your voice matters, your
prayers matter, your tears matter—but the weight of
the battle is Mine, not yours.

Although your intentions are good, at times you are motivated more by fear than love. Let My perfect love drive out all of your fear. Bring the ones you love to Me. Allow Me to surround them and fill them and fight for them. Allow Me alone to be their God. I have worked through your heart and your words and your hands in their lives before, and I will again, but there are some things only I can do. Release them to Me. Rest in Me. Most of all, trust Me. I won't fail you—and I won't fail the ones you love.

When it comes to those we love, we can be very protective. It is often easier to endure heartache ourselves than to see those we love go through a difficult time. Our natural tendency is to try to help; to intervene. This can take many forms depending on the circumstances, but any of our attempts to intervene that are driven more by fear than love are doomed to fail.

Whether it is the fear of watching someone get hurt, fear of loss, fear of the unknown, fear of failure, or even our own fears of being misunderstood or rejected—when our attempts to reach out are rooted in fear, they often bring about the very thing we tried to avoid. But His perfect love really does drive out fear. He is the only One who sees each situation perfectly and knows exactly how to respond.

Release your burdens to the One who loves you—*and* those you love—fully and perfectly. Release them to the only One who can bring about the purest good for their lives. As you let go of your own need to do "something," you're free to watch the miracle of perfect Love unfold in ways you never expected.

Lord, let Your perfect love reveal and dispel all fear as we release those we love to Your faithful care. Thank You for Your perfect, faithful love— for me and for those I love! ~Amen.

Day 10

But seek first his kingdom and his righteousness,
and all these things will be given to you as well.

—Matthew 6:33

You will always do well, beloved, when you seek first the rule and reign of My kingdom. Never allow others to sway your heart and focus away from My priorities for your life and onto what they consider to be more "practical" matters. When your priority is My kingdom, and the things I've personally called you to, you'll know no lack.

While others may be more concerned about security and material comforts, that is not the lifestyle I've called you to. There is nothing wrong with making practical plans for the future, but never allow those plans to trump the stirring of My Spirit within your heart. Never allow human reasoning to move you from a position of faith. And never follow the voice of another, My love—follow Me. You know Me. You hear Me. Trust Me to lead you. Trust Me to sanctify and correct your course if you step out into overzealousness or presumption. But, please, don't allow the fear of getting it wrong to paralyze you and steal your sense of adventure and childlike trust. Even if you do run ahead of Me, I will always be there to catch you. Prioritize the righteousness of My kingdom above all else and you'll find that everything you need is added to you—even when you don't feel like you got everything exactly right.

It sounds so simple, doesn't it? Seek first the kingdom of God. So why does it sometimes feel so complicated? Perhaps it's because "seeking first His kingdom" is often counter-intuitive to the ways of the world. Not only is it counter-intuitive to the ways of the world, it can also be counter to the very sincere and logical counsel of those who love us.

It is always wise to consider the counsel of trusted advisors, but if their guidance contradicts what you know to be God's leading for your life—follow Him. In our overzealousness, can we run ahead or miss Him at times? Sure. But personally I would rather take a risk for the kingdom and fail, than face the greater risk of missing His very best for my life.

Lord thank You for the promises in Your word. Help me to never fear stepping out in faith, because You know the thoughts and intentions of My heart. When my heart is set on following You and seeking first the righteousness of Your kingdom, You will always be faithful to provide everything I need—even if I should fail. ~ Amen.

Day 11

Let patience have its perfect work that you may
be perfect and complete, lacking nothing.

—James 1:4 (NKJV)

*B*eloved, please remember that My love is
patient and My love is kind. My love is
patient and kind toward you. When I ask you
to allow patience to have its perfect work in you, I'm
not asking you to try to squeeze patience out of yourself
in areas and situations where it is clear you have none.
What I am asking is that you allow My patient, kind
love to have its perfect work within you. When My
patient love overcomes your fears, you will find patience
flowing from you in every situation as a naturally
supernatural result of My life flowing through your
own.

You'll never become more patient by trying harder. That hasn't worked out so well for you so far, has it? Instead, remember and acknowledge the reality of your life hidden in Mine. Lean into My peace. Lean into My joy. And especially, lean into My love. Because My love is always there—patiently waiting for you.

Aren't you glad God never asks you to "fake it 'til you make it?" He knows our abilities, and especially our inabilities, better than we know them ourselves.

I don't know about you, but when it comes to this thing called patience—especially patience with things in my life that could use some, um, attention—I need a lot of help. Fortunately He doesn't just help, He takes over! The things I can never do on my own are *already* accomplished *in* Him. And when I learn to lean into the joy and peace I already have in Him—in *every* situation— I've often found patience taking over without even thinking about it. Now, *that* is what I call patience having its perfect work!

Thank You Jesus, for Your patient and kind love. Please continue to let patience have its perfect work in me until I am "perfect and complete, lacking nothing!" ~Amen.

Day 12

The Lord is close to the brokenhearted.

—Psalm 34:18

*C*ome sit with Me, beloved. Crawl up into My lap and rest Your weary head on my chest. Let me hold your hand—and your heart—and let's just be still, together, for a moment. Cry with Me for a while. I don't mind at all. In fact, I love sharing the deep places of your heart. It especially moves Me that so much of your pain comes from sharing the deep places in Mine. The intimacy of our shared heartbreak and longing means so much more to Me than you will ever fathom.

I know you've long understood that I draw near to you in your own heartbreak, but I also long for those *who dare to draw near to Me in Mine. No, it's not easy—you know I never promised it would be—but I did promise I would be with you. And I am. I'm here for you, beloved—now and always.*

Thank You for also being here with Me. Let's weep together for just a moment. I know it often looks like the darkness is winning, but this isn't the end of the story. Weeping endures for a night, but—I promise— joy will come in the morning.

I'm so grateful for the tender loving heart of our Father. He really does draw near to the brokenhearted. He understands in a way no one else can. It is always so tempting to escape our sorrows in a myriad of unhealthy ways—but nothing brings true comfort like crawling up into His lap and actually sharing them *with Him.*

What's even better—and often much harder—is sharing in His own sorrows. There really is a deep intimacy that comes from the authentic fellowship of shared suffering—and it flows both ways.

So wherever you're at right now, and whatever is heavy on your heart, share your struggles with

Him. He is nearer than you think. And after you've shared your heart with Him—take a moment to ask Him what *He* wants to share with *you*.

Lord, thank You for allowing me to share the deepest parts of my heart with You. And thank You even more for trusting me with the deep places in Yours. ~Amen.

Day 13

For we are God's handiwork, created in Christ Jesus to do good works, which God prepared in advance for us to do.

—Ephesians 2:10

I love you, beloved. I love the unique you—the one-of-a-kind you that I created you to be. You were made for love and as you become more and more secure in My love, you will begin to see the unique and personal ways I work in your life. I have purposes for your life that far exceed anything you've ever hoped or imagined. And My plans for you are always good! You are perfect and complete in Me—you lack nothing.

Never compare your life to anyone else's life—only you can be you. And I like you! It's true that there are many, many differences in life circumstances from one person to the next, but always remember that only you have absolutely everything it takes to be you. You have everything you need to fulfill your part in My plans and purposes—a part no one else can ever fill. Even your unique challenges and heartbreaks are redeemed in My presence. Often those are the very things that allow you to display the goodness of My grace to the world around you in personally profound ways.

Your life is a sweet and pleasing aroma to Me, beloved—don't despise what I love. Even your deepest places of weakness and failure are simply invitations to lean into My strength. Be you, My love—you'll find that you're very good at it. And in that place of truth and authenticity—you'll always find My grace to be sufficient.

You're one of a kind. Really! We all know that in theory, but sometimes it's hard to imagine that God really did create each of us individually and uniquely. When we fail to fully embrace who we are in Him—we deny the world the joy of seeing that specific glimpse of *His* heart and character. Despite all our unique traits, we are each still created *in His image.*

I long ago realized that the only thing I will ever be the very best at is being me. When I let go of trying to meet other's expectations—and especially when I let go of trying to meet my *own* expectations—I find tremendous peace and freedom in that place of authenticity. What's more, there is always sufficient grace and strength to simply be who I am.

There's grace for you too. So let go and live *your* life—you're the best you there will ever be!

Father, thank You for creating me in such a way that I can uniquely reflect the beauty of Your face to those around me. Help me to fully embrace everything You've created me to be. May all the unique circumstances of my life even the very hardest things—continuously point to your glorious redemptive nature. ~Amen.

Day 14

We love Him because He first loved us.

—I John 4:19

*D*o you know the way you move My heart, beloved one? Do you know how much I love to be with you; how much I long to hold you close? When you keep yourself at arms distance because of some perceived sense of unworthiness, you don't honor Me—you deprive Me of the intimacy I long to share with you.

I know you do love Me, beloved, and the mere thought of your love thrills My heart and fills me with unspeakable joy. I created you for love—to be loved by Me and to love Me in return. When you allow yourself to receive My love, you're not being selfish or weak, you *are allowing Me the pleasure of doing what I love to do. And I love to love you!*

I know you desire to love Me and others well—and I'm glad that is so—but you can't give away what you don't have. The depth of love you have to give to Me and others is directly related to how much of My love you allow yourself to receive. But even more than that, I want you to receive My love as a simple act of faith and trust, knowing it is My delight and pleasure to share it with you.

Lay aside your many ways of trying to earn My love and simply receive My love for no other reason than the fact that I love to love you. Open your hands, open your heart, breathe deeply and drink from the vast ocean of My love. When you do, you move My heart in ways that are beyond your comprehension. What's more, you give Me one of the greatest gifts a Father could ever receive—the opportunity to pour My own life into the life of My beloved and cherished child.

What a strange and wonderful thought—to think we can actually *move* the heart of God! To think that He *longs* to love us, simply because He loves to love. To think that we actually deprive Him of His desire when we don't allow ourselves to receive His love and affections.

We're just not wired to think that way. We're usually so focused on how we feel and how we're doing that we don't take the time to stop and realize how much *He* enjoys being with us and how much He enjoys loving us—whatever that may look like to each one of us individually.

Our God is the perfect Father and He has no greater joy than seeing His children walk in truth. And *this* is the truth: *You* are a dearly loved child who brings great joy to the heart of your Father. You move His heart—and He absolutely *loves* to love you!

Thank You Lord, for the unfathomable riches of Your love. Help me to receive more and more of Your love-that I might have more love to lavish right back upon You. ~Amen.

Day 15

The LORD doesn't see things the way you see them. People judge by outward appearance, but the LORD looks at the heart.

—I Samuel 16:7

*H*old your head high, beloved. When you give Me your best—whatever that looks like—you've done well. The fragrance of your offering is sweet and pleasing to Me. You've given Me your all and that's all I've ever asked or desired.

Yes, there will always be minor exterior blemishes in even your very best efforts, but all of your imperfection and weakness is swallowed up in My perfection and strength. Your imperfection is made perfect in My presence.

Don't compare your best to anyone else's best. Don't compare your best to your own desires or expectations. You're looking at the outside—I'm looking at your heart. Where you see failure and imperfection, I see the flawless beauty of a heart after my own.

I never release the light of My presence to expose your imperfections, but rather to expose the areas of your heart that have not yet been made perfect in the knowledge of My love. It is My perfect love that covers your every imperfection. It is My perfect love that casts away all of your fears—including your fears of rejection and failure. Because My love never fails.

Rest secure in my acceptance, beloved. Rest secure in my love. Rest secure, because your heart is Mine. This fact alone is always what pleases Me most.

I don't think I will ever grow accustomed to the unfathomable kindness and absolute unconditional acceptance of God. It shouldn't surprise me anymore that He doesn't look at things the way I do—but it still does!

Often I find myself incredibly disappointed with the results of even my very best efforts, but that is never how God feels. He never focuses on the blemishes of my offerings to Him, but He does look with great delight upon the motive and intentions of my heart. And when it gets right down to it, my heart is really all He wants anyway.

There is no way to offer extravagance to the One who is worthy of more than we can ever hope to give, so instead do what you can. Give Him your heart. When you do, it brings Him greater pleasure than you will likely ever fathom.

Thank You Lord, for seeing beyond the imperfections of my outward efforts. Let me rest securely in the reality of Your delight in a heart that simply seeks after Your own. ~Amen.

Day 16

That in the coming ages he might show the incomparable riches of his grace, expressed in his kindness to us in Christ Jesus.

—Ephesians 2:7

*B*eloved, you've long known the sufficiency of My grace—you've spoken of it, you've believed it, you've faithfully stood on its truth. But now I'm inviting you to simply watch and receive as I reveal a new depth of My grace that far exceeds anything you have yet to taste or even fathom.

I am about to impart to you a far deeper understanding of the incomparable riches of this grace I have so freely lavished upon you. Saying "My grace is sufficient" will no longer be a declaration of faith and truth to help you stand firm in the midst of *opposition—rather it will be a shout of praise proclaiming the unfathomable riches of My abundance to you! You've done well, little one, to faithfully lay hold of grace, but now watch and see as My super-abounding grace lays hold of you.*

Grace. Always wonderful, always sufficient, always amazing, grace. Where would we be without grace? It's by grace we're saved. It's by grace we stand. It's by grace that we're held together. And it is grace that will ultimately lead us home. But do we really understand grace? I mean, do we *really* get it? I don't know that I do.

I love grace. I've laid hold of grace. I've embraced grace and I *need* grace. But I'm not entirely sure I truly *understand* the *abounding riches* of grace He has lavished upon us *in* Christ. And I'm not sure I ever will—*except by grace.*

I'm so glad, because that means I can't do anything to earn a greater revelation of grace. I can only *receive* it. I can only receive it as a child— simply opening up my heart and hands before a kind and loving Father. A Father who *always* longs to do so much *more* than I can hope or even imagine.

I have long counted on God to meet my needs–and He has never failed me—but I feel Him tugging on my heart to believe Him for more of my *wants.* Today I'm simply taking Him at His word and opening my heart, just a bit wider, to the One who does immeasurably *more* than all I can ever ask or dream.

Abba, I want a greater revelation of the incomparable riches of Your grace. I don't just need grace—I want a greater revelation of grace that goes far beyond what is necessary and sufficient. I want to know the riches of Your super-abounding grace. I want every single blessing and gift it cost You so dearly to purchase for me. So I come to you as I am. And who I am is Your child. And this child is opening her heart and hands to receive Your grace in ways I never have before. ~Amen.

Day 17

If we are faithless, He remains faithful, for He
cannot deny Himself.

—2 Timothy 2:13

*ave I ever failed you, beloved? When you
look at your circumstances with natural
eyes, you feel as though your faith
is beginning to drift, but I will come through for you
whether you remain strong and steadfast or whether you
waiver. I cannot deny Myself—and I will not deny you.*

*I love you cherished one—I love you when you
stand firm and I love you just as much when you believe
you are faltering. Nothing you do will ever keep Me
from being who I am. But when you forget—for a
moment—to set your gaze and hope fully upon Me,
you sacrifice the peace available to you in that moment.*

I never take My peace from you, but each time you focus on something other than truth, you fail to lay hold of all I've made available to you.

Feelings alone never define your faith. Feeling as though you may not be as focused as you think you ought to be does not mean you lack faith. In fact, fearing you will somehow let Me down by your supposed lack of faithfulness is a lie that causes you to lose sight of the fullness of who you are in Me.

It's true, even if you are faithless I will remain faithful. But know this: You are not faithless! You are here. You are listening for My voice. You want to please Me. You love Me—and I know it. I'm here, too, beloved. I'm always right here with you, regardless of how faithful you do or do not feel. I will never leave you and I will never fail you. But even more importantly, know this—you will never fail Me.

I often make things harder than they need to be, but God's incredible kindness and faithful love always seems to gently woo me back to a place of simple trust. It is always such a relief when I allow myself, again, to rest in His love and in *His* opinion of me.

My feelings change with the wind, but my faith isn't about my feelings. My faith is rooted in the reality of who He is and who I am in Him. I can remain secure in these unchanging facts regardless of how I feel in any given moment.

I'm glad He is forever faithful even if I'm faithless, but I'm even more glad that I'm *not* faithless. If you're reading these words, chances are—neither are you!

Thank You Lord, for seeing beyond the imperfections of my outward efforts. Let me rest securely in the reality of Your delight. And the reality is that one of Your greatest delights is a heart that simply seeks after Your own. ~Amen .

Day 18

"My sheep listen to my voice."

—John 10:27

You hear Me, beloved. You hear Me more often and in more ways than you even imagine. Just as a child learns to understand and speak the language of their parents, you are learning to understand and speak My language—the language of the Spirit.

Sometimes you have believed you were hearing Me less because I haven't continued to speak to you in the same manner I have in the past. When you were first learning to hear My voice, you needed assurances and confirmations that I no longer provide, because you no longer need them in the same way. But you are still leaning in to listen and that makes My heart glad!

Many are unwilling, or unable, to press in deeper and move beyond their familiar belief systems, but that is not true of you. I am so pleased by your simple decision to trust My heart even when you are not able to clearly discern My voice.

I withhold no good thing from you, My love. I am always drawing you deeper—hiding treasure for you and never from you. It thrills My heart that you have come to a place where you trust My faithfulness far more than you trust your own experience of how I have led you in the past.

Even now, I am speaking to you, beloved—heart to heart, and spirit to spirit—in a depth of communion beyond anything mere words could convey. As a father delights in watching his child's understanding grow and unfold, I have had the great delight of watching you grow in wisdom and understanding as you've learned to "hear" in ways few ever do.

God's first language isn't English. And no, it isn't Hebrew either! It is the language of the Spirit. We often limit ourselves in our capacity to "hear" Him because we try to hear Him in ways that make sense to us. We filter what He is communicating through the methods we already understand and are familiar with. But there is so much more!

God is an excellent communicator. He already understands our language, He wants us to lean into His heart so we can learn His. Ask Him to teach you. Lay your head on His chest like John did and rest His presence. Meditate on His word. Be still and know He is God. You just may be surprised to learn you "hear" more in times of silent communion than at any other time. His sheep really do *know* His voice!

Lord, what a privilege it is to lean in to hear Your heart. May we press in more and more to hear the things You want to communicate and not just the things we think we ought to be hearing. ~Amen.

Day 19

"Bring the whole tithe into the storehouse, that there may be food in my house. Test me in this," says the LORD Almighty, "and see if I will not throw open the floodgates of heaven and pour out so much blessing that there will not be room enough to store it."

—Malachi 3:10

I see your desire to honor Me in your finances and that pleases Me, but sometimes your focus is more on satisfying yourself with proof of your faithfulness, than it is on giving with a glad and cheerful heart. Generosity and cheerful giving aren't about numbers, they are about a lifestyle of worship, gratitude, and surrender.

You do well when you are a faithful steward of your financial resources, but you do even better when *you are faithful with the entirety of your life. I don't need your money, but I want all of your heart—and that is what you've given Me.*

I'm inviting you to test Me—to prove Me—when you trust Me with everything. But when you focus on details I'm not focused on—when you wonder if maybe you haven't given absolutely everything you could possibly have given—you're trying to prove yourself, not Me.

I love you, little one. I love the earnestness of your heart. I love your desire to withhold nothing. But in your zeal you sometimes miss the point. It has never been about getting all the details just right, it is about the heart. It is about giving Me your heart then trusting Me to do what I've already promised to do.

So test Me in this and see if I will not throw open the floodgates of heaven with so much blessing you cannot contain it!

Giving God control of our financial resources is good and necessary, but giving Him control of our hearts and lives is even better.

I struggled financially for many years. There were lots of reasons—some outside of my control, and some I probably could have "controlled" a bit better. One result during this time was that I never seemed to be able to give as much as I wanted to give. Although I did often stretch myself in this area, especially when I felt the Lord was challenging me to trust Him at a new level, somehow I always thought I should be able to do more. That is until the Lord schooled me on *what* He was really after and *who* He really wanted me to prove (hint: it wasn't me!).

Well, He did "prove" Himself in the specific situation I was facing and let's just say He's proved Himself time and again since then. He'll prove Himself to you too. Give Him your all and watch those floodgates open!

Lord, it's really true—we can never out-give You! Teach us to be cheerful, generous givers of our resources—and, especially, of our hearts and lives ~Amen.

Day 20

See, I am doing a new thing! Now it springs up;
do you not perceive it? I am making a way in the
wilderness and streams in the wasteland.

—Isaiah 43:19

*I*t's a new day and I am doing a new thing!
Now it springs up! Not soon, but now. Right
here, right now, I am doing a new thing—in
your life and also in the world around you.

The coming season won't be a new page, or a new
chapter, but a whole new storyline. Although
everything in the past has served to prepare you for this
season, you cannot imagine how the story will unfold.
You will watch in wonder as I put the pieces together
and create a picture more beautiful than you could have
ever dreamed. In this picture, all the piece of your life

will fit perfectly. You fit, beloved—you have always fit perfectly into My plans and purposes. Now, you will see it in a way you never have before.

I know how tempting it has been to grow weary in the waiting, but you stood firm. You continued to believe. You trust Me now more than ever—and you will see your faith become sight.

This season is different than any season you've experienced before, so your mind can't conceive all your spirit is already sensing. But that's a good thing! Lean into Me. Leave the disappointments of yesterday in the past—and watch with anticipation and wonder as this new seasons unfolds. Don't remember the former things—it's a whole new day!

There is change in the air. God is doing a new thing. His mercies are new *every* day, but there are certain times when *everything* changes. There are certain dates with destiny and certain times of divine convergence. In those times, we need to cling to Him more than ever!

Every change brings both blessing and challenge. Focus on the blessing, but don't be caught off guard by the challenges. Focus on what is coming, not what has been. It will all be worth it!

"Eye has not seen, ear has not heard, mind cannot conceive what God has prepared for those who love Him!" His blessings are always worth the wait!

Father thank You for the excitement and expectation of new days and new seasons. Prepare me for all You have in store! ~Amen.

Day 21

Turn away my eyes from looking at worthless
things, and revive me in Your way.

—Psalm 119:37 (NKJV)

*L*ook up, beloved—and keep looking up. I
know your heart is discouraged and you're
not sure where to turn, but before you turn to
the right or to the left, turn again to me. I see you. I see
the confusion and the challenges before you. I feel the
heaviness in your heart, but I'm still right here with
you. I haven't left you. I haven't forgotten you—and I
never will.

I will revive your heart again as you turn your eyes from the perplexities of your current circumstances and fix them steadfastly on Me. There is nothing to be gained by focusing on disappointment and doubt, but much to be gained by taking your place seated with Me in heavenly realms. There your perspective will be realigned with Mine. There your outlook will change and the fog will clear. And there, secure in your rightful place as My child—as My beloved—your heart will be strengthened, your soul will be refreshed, and your mind will be at peace. Revived in My ways, you'll know when to wait, when to move forward—and you'll always know which way to turn.

Have you ever noticed that it is impossible to feel hopeless when gazing into the eyes of Jesus? When we turn away from a focus on the perplexities and challenges of life and instead fix our eyes steadfastly on Him, our perspective on everything changes.

According to Paul (in Ephesians 2:6), we are, present-tense, seated in heavenly realms *with* Christ. We are not left to our own limited resources. We are not confined to our own limited perspective. We have everything we need right now *in* Him. But in order to dial into that remarkable reality, sometimes we need to intentionally shift our focus *away* from the inferior reality of the temporary trials of this present moment, and *onto* the superior reality of our exceedingly abundant eternal inheritance. No other single action will make a greater difference in your "now."

Lord, please, turn our eyes from the challenges of life and revive us in Your ways! Thank You, Jesus, for the abundant inheritance we have in You—help us to bring that reality into our now by purposefully aligning our hearts and perspective with Your own. Teach us Your ways Lord, so we will confidently walk in the reality of who we are in You. ~Amen.

Day 22

For no matter how many promises God has made,
they are "Yes" in Christ. And so through him the
"Amen" is spoken by us to the glory of God.

—1 Corinthians 1:20

Yes. That is My answer, beloved, yes. All of My promises in your life are still yes. I haven't changed My mind. You haven't missed My plan. I am faithful to finish all I've begun.

I know you think that because certain things haven't worked out the way you thought they would, it means some of My promises are no longer meant for you. Nothing could be further from the truth. Each step of faith you've taken matters! Each choice to believe and to risk has brought you closer to the ultimate fulfillment of My purposes for your life. There will always be mystery in the journey and there will always be things you cannot explain and things that will not fit within your understanding. But I will prove Myself faithful to you—of that you can be sure.

How is it possible I could forget you, My child? I see you wondering if your mistakes—both real and imagined—have disqualified you. But I don't view your life the way you do. I am a rewarder of those who diligently seek Me—period. And you, My love, have diligently sought Me. Through the desert, through the long days of disappointment, through misunderstanding and mystery—you have continued to seek My face. Tell Me, what could possibly give My heart more pleasure than to know you trust Me even when nothing has made sense?

Yes, beloved, yes. All of My promises are still yes. You need only agree with Me. Add your "amen" to My "yes" and together we'll change the world.

God isn't just the Alpha, He is the Omega. He's not just the Promise-Giver, He is the Promise-Keeper. Nothing will thwart His purposes—and nothing will keep Him from completing all He has begun in Your life.

Regardless of how many seeming setbacks and delays you have experienced, God is still up to good in your life. His promises to you are still "yes"—so keep saying "amen" and watch His great faithfulness unfold!

Thank You Jesus for Your faithfulness. You are the Author and Finisher, You are the Alpha and Omega. God, You know my heart like no other—please give me the grace to continue to trust You more. Give me the perseverance to keep seeking You in every season with full assurance that You will complete all You've begun. ~Amen.

Day 23

He brought me to the banqueting house, and his banner over me was love.

—Song of Solomon 2:4

You are my first choice. You are My best thought. You have never been second in My heart and you are never an afterthought. I chose you to be Mine before you ever knew My name. And I chose you just as you are. I will never give or withhold My love based on your performance. I am never disinterested in you, or the things you have to say. I am never distracted when you call out to Me—I'm never too busy and I never have more important things to do.

You are the object of My affection and the desire of My heart. I love it when you tell Me your dreams and desires; I love it when you share all that's in your heart;

I even love it when you sit with Me in silence because you have no words left to say. I promise to never disconnect from you, My love—My arms and My heart are always open and I will never push you away. Draw near to Me, because I've already drawn near to you.

My banner over you is love. Always love. Only love. Forever, My highest thought for you is love—I chose and created you for love. My love for you is patient and kind. My love for you is perfect and pure. My love for you endures. And because My love endures—My love for you is now.

Now and forever, I pledge My love to you. I pledge My faithfulness to you. I promise to be so very careful with your heart—especially with all the tender places of loss and disappointment. I will never betray your trust. Never. I am yours, and you are Mine. You are My first choice—and I chose you for love.

Isn't that an amazing thought? You are God's first choice. He never wanted *anyone* more than He wants you. Even if it seems like you are constantly overlooked by others, you are never overlooked by God.

In these days of overly crowded lives and schedules, it is so refreshing to realize your name is always on God's calendar and that He is always available to you. There may be distractions galore in your life but He is never distracted from His steadfast focus on you. He is always waiting for you. In fact, He's waiting right now. So don't wait a moment longer. Share all that's on your heart as you turn your attention to the One whose full attention is *always* on you.

Lord, thank You for the crazy amazing reality of Your love. I am My Beloved's and He is mine! Thank You, God, for choosing me first, for loving me first—and for loving me always. ~Amen.

Day 24

Hope deferred makes the heart sick, but a
longing fulfilled is a tree of life.

—Proverbs 13:12

*am the God of hope and I alone am the source
of your hope. Even when the fulfillment of your
dreams and desires takes longer than you would
like, that doesn't mean hope itself is deferred. When
you believe Me and know My faithfulness, hope is alive
even as you wait.*

*I will prove myself faithful to you, beloved. When
you cling to that truth in every season, you will find
yourself filled with joy and peace as you believe through
the power of My spirit. Hope is not dependent upon
answers, hope is dependent upon faith. Faith in Me.
Faith in My character. Faith in My ability to do what*

you cannot. Faith in My ability to sustain you, prepare you, and fulfill you.

Trust Me, little one. Trust My intentions. I know waiting sometimes makes your heart feel sick, but when you focus on the truth—the truth of My love and good intentions for your life—rather than losing heart, you will look forward in the confident expectation of good. And one day very soon, you will look around and be astounded at the depth of rich fulfillment flowing through your life.

Hope is such a precious commodity. During long seasons of waiting and what seems like ongoing delays in seeing your deepest desires become reality, it is often tempting to give in to the temptation of heartsickness and hopelessness. But He is the God of hope and His hope *never* disappoints. Even when your dreams seem to be a long time in coming, or when they are rearranged beyond recognition, you *never* need to postpone your hope. Because only those who hope in the Lord gain *new* strength. So go ahead and get your hopes up—again and again and again—because those who trust in Him will *never* be put to shame.

God of hope, fill me with Your joy and peace that I might abound in hope through the power of the Holy Spirit. It's not something I can conjure up, but something Your Spirit freely gives. I choose not to defer my hope, instead I will hope in You, Lord, knowing that as I do—You will renew my strength and fulfill Your promises. ~Amen.

Day 25

So do not throw away your confidence; it will
be richly rewarded.

—Hebrews 10:35

I am the Promise Giver, and I am the Promise Keeper. I see you growing anxious and searching for someone, anyone, to confirm the promises I have spoken over your life. But beloved, isn't enough that I have spoken? My word has spoken. And what I have spoken, I will do.

Many times I will send My people to confirm a word over your life, and many times I bring My body around you to offer great encouragement. But there are times you need to choose to believe even in the absence of any significant encouragement. There are times you need to decide what you really believe—what you believe about Me, and what you believe about My intentions toward you.

You hear My voice, beloved. You've heard My heart for you. You've heard the sweet whispers of My love and encouragement—directly from My heart to your own. While I love to see My children encourage each other in love, there are times I reserve that privilege for Myself. There are things I want to speak to you personally. I want to experience the joy of your deepened trust in Me. And as you learn to trust, I want to build your confidence—confidence in who you already know I've called and created you to be.

I will never fail you, beloved. I keep My promises. So hold onto your confidence—it will be richly rewarded.

In seasons of uncertainty, have you ever turned to a friend, or mentor, or even a greatly respected spiritual leader, hoping for the perfect encouraging word to jump-start your lagging faith? Often God does encourage us in this way and it's a marvelous expression of the Body of Christ building each other up in love. But other times—sometimes even during our most difficult seasons of testing—it seems like there is nothing but crickets when you're aching for that little nugget of encouragement. Or worse, you turn to someone you think will understand, and they actually make you feel worse. It's not that they don't care, or don't want to help, but sometimes God simply hasn't given them the revelation to speak accurately into your current situation.

When you find yourself in this situation, it is usually because there is something else going on beneath the surface. And, that "something else"— just might be God nudging you along into a place of deeper trust and confidence. Hang on to what you know to be true, my friend, because He will *never* fail you.

Father, thank You for your faithfulness and for giving me opportunities to trust You! Help me to remember who You are and all that You've promised. And, especially, please help me to hold onto my confidence in You. ~Amen.

Day 26

"It is finished!"

—John 19:30

*C*ome closer, beloved. The veil has been torn. The door is standing wide open. I've made a way for you to come boldly into My presence. Come closer. There is nothing stopping you. The only thing that can keep us apart is your own unbelief. Don't punish yourself by allowing your perceived inadequacies to keep you from My love. When you fail, or feel stuck, or undisciplined, or whatever, it doesn't affect what I think about you, but it often affects what you think about you. And what you think about you affects how much of My grace you allow yourself to access. I am still both the Author and Finisher of your *faith. Your part is to simply agree with what I've already declared—and with what I've already accomplished.*

It is finished! Nothing you do—good or bad—can add to, or take away from, what I already purchased with My own blood. Come closer, beloved. Rest your weary head on My shoulder. Lean into the patience and kindness that is always in My heart for you. Allowing foolish guilt and condemnation to keep you from My embrace, not only keeps you feeling burdened and weighed down, it also deprives Me of your cherished companionship. Come closer, beloved—because I want to be with you.

If we were to be honest, most of us have times when we think the Good News is just a little too good to actually be true. We know our own imperfections and weaknesses and tend to think there is a point, especially in repeated areas of struggle, where maybe we've worn out God's grace. We feel like maybe we can't bring *that* to Him again because we've already failed so many times. We begin to push Him away–maybe just a little–because we don't feel worthy of such great mercy and kindness. But guess what? It's not about how *you* feel, it's about what *He's* done–and it *is* finished! For real. The Good News really is *that* good! Our sin really is *all* forgiven–no matter how many times we miss the mark. There's no penance to pay. No hoops to jump through. Just open arms waiting the moment you turn in His direction. And oh how He longs for you to turn in His direction! So go ahead–get closer. Get as close as you want. He's waiting there for you. In fact, He's longing for you to come.

Thank You Lord, for good news! Thank You for the finished work of the cross and for the mercy that always covers me. Thank You, especially, for the love that draws me near—again and again and again. ~Amen

Day 27

Now to him who is able to do immeasurably more
than all we ask or imagine, according to his
power that is at work within us, to him be glory
in the church and in Christ Jesus throughout all
generations, forever and ever! Amen

—Ephesians 3:20-21

I *want you to behold the immense power and
splendor of the ocean, beloved. I want you to
consider the breathtaking beauty and vastness of
a starlit sky. As you observe these wonders, know that
they don't begin to measure the vastness of My love for
you. They don't begin to display the greatness of My
power that is at your disposal. They don't begin to
display the beauty of the thoughts I think toward you,*

or the great joy I have when I imagine the wonderful future I have dreamed for you.

You are allowing the past to obscure your vision of the future, little one. My vision for you is limitless. Lean into Me. Lean into My endless resources and My boundless grace. Stop measuring your success by what you see with your natural eyes, or by the standards of the world. You are not of this world—You a citizen of My eternal, limitless kingdom.

I want you to set aside your fears and begin to dream again. I want you to dream with Me. I want you to create with Me. I want you to believe that My plans for you really are good—so good that they are immeasurably beyond anything you can even ask or imagine!

Will you dream with Me, beloved? My heart is longing to soar with yours.

It's strange to think that God *wants* us to dream. But He does! He created us for so much more than most of us even dare to imagine. In fact, His plans for us are so good, they are *beyond* anything we can imagine!

As glorious as that sounds, most of us have a hard time actually believing it. We all experience bumps in life. We all experience loss, disappointment, and delays. When that happens, it is easy to "dumb-down" our dreams and begin to settle for less than what our heart truly desires.

But what if God really means what He says? What if His plans really are beyond our wildest imagination? What if His limitless resources really are at our disposal? Wouldn't it be worth pushing past our fears to find out?

Go ahead and dream. Go ahead and trust the One who is so very careful with your heart. Just don't be surprised if you find yourself soaring beyond the stars!

Lord, thank You for the invitation to dream. God, you know my desires. Help me to dream beyond my fears and beyond my past. Your plans for me are for good—to give me hope and a glorious future. I choose to trust You, Lord. And, secure in the knowledge of Your love, I also choose to dream. ~Amen .

Day 28

"Come, follow me," Jesus said.

—Mark 1:17

Follow Me, beloved. Leave your striving. Leave your need for answers and a carefully crafted plan. Leave behind every lesser pursuit and simply come—come and follow Me.

I see the ache in your heart for a return to simplicity. I know you long to let go of the things that distract you and bring unnecessary complexity to your life. But it's not so difficult as you sometimes imagine. Each time I call out to you, I always release the grace to respond. All you need to do is listen—and then simply follow.

I love you. I love being with you. I love walking through life with you. I love it when you reach for My hand like a trusting child and simply allow Me lead.

Follow Me, beloved. Follow as I lead you. Never compare your path to that of another. You, follow Me. Never allow preconceived ideas of how I should be leading you delay your willingness to follow. Follow Me when the way is clear, and follow Me when the path is shrouded in mystery. Follow Me and do only what you see Me doing. As you do, I promise to guide you and teach you My ways. I promise to never leave you. I promise to never fail you.

Simply follow Me, beloved, and the simplicity you crave will soon be following you.

I don't know about you, but my heart craves simplicity. When I read the Gospels and witness how Jesus called His first disciples, my own heart is filled with longing—a longing to simply follow Him. To follow Him with no excuses, no delays, no negotiations, and no agenda. The disciples heard His voice and accepted His invitation—period.

I can't help but think our lives would be simpler—maybe *much* simpler—if we learned to do the same. If we learned to simply follow. So that's what I'm going to do. I'm going to watch. I'm going to wait. I'm going to listen. And when He calls again (and He always does)—I'm going to simply follow.

Jesus I'm so grateful for the beautiful and simple privilege of following You. I'm so thankful that following You doesn't need to be complicated. Lord help me listen for Your voice and respond to Your invitation without hesitation. I can trust Your leadership, Lord, so I choose to follow. I choose to simply follow all the days of my life. ~Amen.

Day 29

He who dwells in the secret place of the Most
High, shall abide under the shadow
of the Almighty

—Psalm 91:1 (NKJV)

*I*n secret—in the quiet stillness of a new day—I
am working. You can trust Me, beloved. My
hands are those of a skilled Master Potter, and
with those hands, I am forming and transforming your
heart.

I'm answering your prayers, My love. But I know
you never expected it to look or feel quite like this. Will
you trust Me? Even in this place of uncertainty and
pain, will you surrender your heart and expectations to
Me? I won't let you go, and I won't fail you.

You asked Me to open your eyes—and I did. You asked Me to share My heart—and I did. I know things that once seem simple and clear, no longer make sense. I know your heart has been broken by things few understand. But I am holding you in the palm of My hand. I have hidden you under the shadow of My wing. And there, in secret, you will learn, again, that My grace is absolutely sufficient.

Thank you for being willing to share My heart for those enslaved in deepest darkness, but I didn't create you to carry burdens beyond your ability to bear. Share them with Me, then rest in the knowledge that I alone can carry what you cannot. Rest in the knowledge that the darkness has already been defeated and that I will arise in justice and righteousness on behalf of the poor and oppressed. Rest in the knowledge that My love always wins.

I have more for you to do, little one. But for just a while longer rest here with Me in the secret place. Rest here, and allow Me to restore your soul.

Truly knowing the heart of God is our greatest privilege. It is also costly. Love is the greatest power in the universe, but in the midst of a broken, fallen world, love can be incredibly painful. That is especially true when faced with some of the deepest depravity on this sin-sick planet, because love is never disengaged.

Being awakened to areas of great pain and suffering—not to mention learning to share the deep aches in God's own heart—will always come at a cost. Learning to see and engage *without* becoming incapacitated by the magnitude of the need is a process. Fortunately, His grace is always sufficient. As we learn to rest fully in His sufficiency and victory, we'll become better able to effectively meet the needs He is personally calling and equipping us to meet.

Abba, thank You for the privilege of sharing Your heart. Lord teach me to love in a way that makes a difference. Thank You for opening my eyes even when the pain of seeing is almost unbearable. As You heal and strengthen my heart, teach me to rest fully in Your sufficiency so I'll have something real to give those around me. ~Amen.

Day 30

Be still and know that I am God.

—Psalm 46:10

ake a moment, My love. Take one brilliant, blissful moment—to breathe. Allow Me to quiet the turmoil of your raging emotions. Let Me show you how to release the strain and stress churning within your soul.

Look up. Look deeply. Look beyond the temporal. Look beyond your circumstances and search My eyes. In My eyes you'll see the truth—You'll know that My eyes are always on you.

Breathe in the beauty of My peace. Fix your gaze upon the glory that fills My kingdom. Know that I hear you each and every time you call—even when your voice is only a faint whisper on the wind. So call out to Me, beloved—it is such sweet music to My ears. Call out and keep calling, until you hear the sound of My heart calling out to yours.

Allow My mercy to hold you. Experience My peace flowing past your understanding as My abounding grace floods every corner of your soul.

I want to comfort you. I want to hold you close. I want to speak to you and calm the fear in your heart. I long to whisper words of encouragement and delight to your soul. So slow down. Take a moment. Take one brilliant, blissful moment—to breathe.

Why is it so hard to be still? There will always be a myriad of distractions vying for our attention, but we don't have to let the distractions win. It only takes a moment—one brilliant blissful moment—to slow down enough to take a deep breath and reconnect. It only takes a moment to step back and reprioritize. It only takes a moment to focus and reset our gaze on the One whose eyes are always on us.

Each and every moment in His presence is a gift. Each and every intimate moment of connection is priceless. Not just to us—but also to Him. Whoever you are, whatever you are doing—the invitation is there. The invitation—from His heart to yours—is *always* there. The invitation to be still. The invitation to come away with Him. The invitation to simply be. He is always just a breath away.

Thank You Jesus for Your blissful invitations to slow down and breathe. Forgive me, Lord, for allowing myself to be drawn away by the distractions of life. Help me to focus, Lord. Thank You for hearing even my faintest whispers for help and for drawing me, again and again, to Your heart. ~Amen.

ABOUT THE AUTHOR

Cindy Powell is the author of several books including *The Key to His Heart*. More recently she released *HR Matters* –a book on human resources for churches and ministries. Whether writing or speaking her desire is that her words will draw others closer to the heart of God. Visit her blog and website at:

www.cindypowell.org

or email:
simplefaith247@gmail.com

For professional information, please visit:

www.cindypowellhr.com

Made in the USA
San Bernardino, CA
05 April 2017